FOREIGNERS
IN CHINA

Compiled by Jiao Bo
Translated by Pan Shuangqin

China Intercontinental Press

Foreword

Lisa Carducci

Once upon a time...

Once upon a time, China was a mystical country: an exotic dream at the ends of the earth; a magnetic pole. China still has a strong attraction, but for different reasons. Today, people from all around the world come here to study, work, and do research. They come to help China develop, and also to prosper, especially since China joined the WTO in December 2001. It was not so long ago that a person who travelled to China was regarded as some kind of hero, and would be introduced: "This is my friend who has been to China, you know..."

China had closed herself off for centuries, content with herself - the Middle Kingdom - and dismissive of everywhere else. Much, much later, a reverse trend occurred: the West knew best; the West was right, good and great. The Chinese nation lost confidence in itself and started to admire and accept all that came from outside. Chinese people formerly saw the world as consisting simply of "we, the Chinese, and you, the foreigners." In addition to being lumped into one category, all foreigners also shared the blanket term "Westerners," even the Japanese! The wider China opens its doors to the external world and the further Chinese people travel abroad, the more aware they become of facial characteristics, and the greater their ability to identify a spoken language. They also realise that not all foreigners are Christians and nor do they all speak English.

An album of this kind represents a precious bridge between various cultures, civilisations and countries, and helps open readers' eyes to our multifaceted world. It includes people from such places as Switzerland, Canada, Pakistan, the Republic of Korea, England, the United States, Sweden, France, Austria, and encompasses men and women, the elderly and the young, all with diverse knowledge, interests and skills. The album is a way of serving up the world on a tray and demonstrating the richness of humankind and the diversity of life, and provides an image of one small part the world. It also shows diversity in the field of activities taken up by foreigners living in China: teachers, diplomatic staff, investors, barmen, hairdressers, models, musicians, sportsmen, chefs, and translators. Some are involved in theatre, medicine, dance, and charitable activities; some are here studying taiji, Peking opera, and acupuncture.

It is now a common discovery on taking a closer look at a group of children playing, laughing and talking together that they come from all countries but China. Yet they speak Chinese with no accent other than the local one, because they were born in China, or came here as infants, and made their first steps on Chinese soil. Their parents leave them with a Chinese ayi when they go to work, and the pale, freckled children with reddish hair and blue eyes from Europe, America and Australia learn Chinese as their mother tongue, as do children with darker skin and hair from Cuba, Sudan, or Bangladesh. The world has no more frontiers, no limits. The Global Village in under construction!

Since Beijing was named host of the 2008 Olympic Games, foreign language learning has become a popular evening, weekend and holiday activity. English is still the favourite, but, to my great pleasure, other languages such as French, Italian, Russian, and Spanish gain popularity. Classes of all kinds are available: intensive, extensive, and even hyper-intensive; standard or brushing-up classes; language for leisure, travel, business or just plain survival.

Among foreigners who that have been here for a long period, even for decades, a large number close themselves off from the Chinese world. They live in their own environment, never make friends with any Chinese, never learn the language, watch only foreign movies, and eat as they do in their own country. In other words, they not only remain foreigners, but also strangers. Others fall in love not only with China but also with a son or a daughter of this country, and tie the knot. The growing number of so-called "overseas marriages" or "international marriages" is a rational consequence of China's opening-up, and indicates a broadening of minds. These couples are accepted in their community, and no longer looked down upon or criticised. For every nine foreign men that marry Chinese women (of an average age 31), one foreign woman marries a Chinese man. In Shanghai, for instance, there were 400 overseas marriages in 1980, but by 2002 this figure had rocketed to 2,705. Between 1996 and 2002, there were 21,015 mixed marriages registered in Shanghai: 40 per cent to Japanese, and 38 per cent to overseas Chinese and spouses from Taiwan, Macao and Hong Kong. The others were from the United States (6.3 percent), Australia (5.4 percent) and European countries (3.9 percent).

Opening-up brings cross-cultural communication. Whether or not a foreigner can be happy in China, or a Chinese in another country, depends on their capacity to adapt. Those who resist their new environment and cherish, defend, and protect their own cultural values in the belief none approaches will suffer and - sooner or later - surrender and die. As an 'expatriate' in China, why not take this marvellous opportunity to make a general spiritual clear-out? Set down all the values, morals, rules, customs, habits of your own country; examine them one by one; compare them with their local equivalents; sort, select and put them back in order in your life. Experience has taught me that this is the only way to happiness.

Finally, I would like to mention the contribution foreigners make to China's economy. I am not talking of investment through official channels, but of more modest, almost imperceptible contributions. Foreigners who live in China for a certain time not only travel across the country (and spend money) but invite their relatives and friends to see with their own eyes this wonderful country they read about in letters and e-mails from their love ones. Attracting foreigners to China achieves more than just economic contributions: it is a cultural contribution that builds a bridge of mutual understanding and friendship between individuals and nations.

When I came to China for the first time in 1985, I could not buy things, eat, or take notes without being surrounded by dozens of Chinese, curious to see what a foreigner would choose at the market, and how much she would be charged according to the length of her nose. They were fascinated as to whether she could use chopsticks, and by the strange 'characters' written on her map of China. They would touch my brown hair, try to guess how old I was, and how many dollars I had in my bag. Today, who, at least in large cities, has not yet seen a foreigner in the flesh? Curiosity is disappearing. Now is the time to learn to live together and cooperate towards building a better world. This is the reason of this book about foreigners in China.

目录
Contents

A Long Life of Affection

© Photos by Dai Shulin

↑ Hucang villagers attending the funeral procession in the rain.
↗ In 1935, the Austrian girl Gertrude Wagner and Du Chengrong at their wedding ceremony in Hangzhou (file photo).

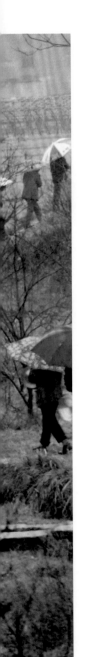

On February 24, 1935, an Austrian girl Gertrude Wagner and a Chinese police officer Du Chengrong held their wedding ceremony in the Hangzhou Xinxin Hotel. At the ceremony, Du Chengrong gave his wife a Chinese name—Hua Zhiping, which means a person met by chance who becomes a bosom friend for life.

Gertrude Wagner and Du Chengrong met and got to know each other in Austria, where the Chinese police officer was undergoing training from 1931 until 1933. At that time, Gertrude's father was Du's instructor. She used to accompany her father to work every day and so got to know the handsome young man. When Du had completed his training course, the 17-year-old Gertrude told her friends: "I will marry a Chinese". Her parents were opposed, but were finally won over by the teenage girl's persistence as she kept insisting: "This is my happiness." In 1935, Gertrude Wagner came to China and became the wife of Du Chengrong.

Between 1935 and 1949, the couple experienced China's War of Resistance Against Japan and the Civil War. During that period, Gertrude gave a birth to four children. In August 1949, Du demobilized and returned to his hometown of Hucang Village in Zhejiang Province with his wife. In the countryside, Gertrude, like other village women, learnt how to raise chickens, ducks and rabbits. She also learnt to cook the local meals, such as baking corn cakes, and to make cotton shoes and other household tasks. In a letter to her younger brother, she wrote: "Here, enjoyment is non-existent and ballet, skiing and ice-skating makes no sense." Life was very hard for her, but Gertrude tried every means to let her children receive good education. In 1952, when her elder son went to senior high school, she sold her gold bracelets that had been left by her mother, and divided the money into three parts—one for her son's tuition fee, another for chemical fertilizers and the other for seeds.

In 1978, China started to implement the reform and opening-up policies, and rural life improved. Unfortunately,

Du was diagnosed with cancer in 1989. He actively cooperated with doctors to treat the disease, as he wanted to accompany his wife in their old age. Although old, Gertrude personally took care of her husband. In April 1990, she got an Austrian nationality certificate. On April 28, the 84-year-old Du was seriously ill and could not speak to express his feelings. But Gertrude could read his heart and showed him the certificate of Austrian nationality. Seeing it, Du closed his eyes, at ease.

It was raining on February 26, 2003. The 86-year-old Gertrude passed away at her home in Hucang Village. Her sons and grandsons buried her with her husband. The whole village took part in the funeral procession. After first meeting at an ice-skating rink in Vienna 68 years ago, Gertrude and Du Chengrong finished their hard but happy life together. "She loved her husband so much and took good care of him. I will never forget the manner in which they spoke to each other," said the executive vice chairman of the Austria-China Friendship Association.

生于一九一六年十二月十七日
卒于二〇〇三年二月十九日

华知萍

With lanterns in hand, inscribed with the Chinese character Du, villagers express their profound condolences over the death of the couple Du Chengrong and Gertrude Wagner.

Wagner leaves the house that she lived in for so many years for the last time.

The Austrian Consul to Shanghai, Ms. Weinberger, meets Gertrude's relatives.

Goodbye Grandma Wagner.

A happy family gathering.
In 2001, Austrian Parliamentary Head Geister meets Gertrude in Zhejiang Province.
A cheerful and optimistic woman.

Howard's China Affection

Photos by Gu Yongwei

↑ Howard marries Xin Lihua in 1956 (selected from the family album).

⇢ The happy family—Howard with his granddaughter.

"War entirely changed my life," said Howard Adams.

Howard, a native of Dallas in Texas, was in the US Army during World War II and the Korean War. After the fighting ended, he stayed in China.

In September 1954, he came to work in a papermaking factory in Jinan, Shandong Province, and soon became a outstanding technician. Two years later, Howard met a Jinan girl named Xin Lihua and married her several months later. Xin's family members all liked him. Xin took good care of her husband, cooking delicious Chinese food for him and teaching him to speak Chinese. Though Howard's income was enough to support the family, the hard-working wife still often went out to do temporary work.

In September 1963, Howard entered the People's University of China (Renmin Daxue) majoring in international politics. At that time, he had a six-year-old daughter named Huo Lide. Howard moved to Beijing with his wife and daughter. As with other foreign students studying in Beijing, Howard lived in a school dormitory. His wife and daughter lived outside the school, and their home soon became a place often visited by students from various countries. The wife's warmth and hospitality made a deep impression on Howard's friends. They said they would marry a Chinese girl like Xin Lihua. In 1969, Howard's family returned to the papermaking factory in Shandong Province.

In 1979, China and the United States officially established diplomatic relations. The next year, Howard's father died in the United States. Howard was saddened by the news. Missing his mother, he quickly returned to the United States. With the Chinese way to express sorry, he knelt for a long time in front of his mother whom he hadn't seen for more than 30 years. Because of the limited conditions, Howard's mother could not come to China with her son and only kept several photos of her daughter-in-law and granddaughter. Three years later, Howard's mother passed away.

After coming back from the United States, Howard worked as a teacher in Shandong Medical Institute (now known as Shandong Medical University). In 1983, Howard's granddaughter Shasha came into this world and brought great happiness to this family. Howard never spoke Chinese with his granddaughter before the age of four, so that she grew up in an English-speaking environment. At the age of four, she was joined by a younger sister, Shaman. So, looking after the two granddaughters became a main work of the old couple in their later years. Howard loved the two children very much and used to take them out by bike.

But, while Shasha and Shaman were growing up, their grandmother's health was deteriorating. To make his wife happy, Howard took her on a three-month trip to Europe. At the end of 1993, the wife died of lung cancer. Missing her, Howard often rides his bicycle to her grave surrounded by mountains and burns incense in front of the tomb while conversing with her.

Every year, Howard's family is selected as a "model family."

The granddaughter likes to have the breakfast cooked by Howard.

Happy with friends.

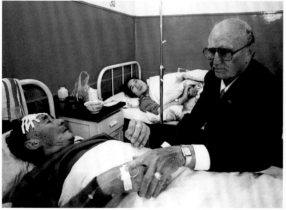

↑ Howard hopes to be buried with his wife after he dies.
"In this way, I can live with my wife," he said.
↑ Howard goes to a hospital to see his basketball coach.
→ Howard's greatest wish is that his granddaughter could
become a ballet dancer.

↑ Every day, Howard keeps doing exercise.

↗ Though his mouth is dry after a long class, Howard still patiently answers question raised by his students.

→ Howard has taught in the Shandong Medical University for nearly 20 years.

Comic Star Dashan

Photos by Wang Wenquan

Ask a Chinese whether he or she knows Mark Rowswell, and the answer will mostly be in the negative. But, if the name was changed to "Dashan", then millions of Chinese people would nod and smile. Almost all families in China know the name of Canadian Dashan, as he performed at a Chinese Spring Festival celebration party not long after he came to China. He became extremely popular because he spoke very standard Chinese and his performance attracted the Chinese audience.

In 1988, while studying at Beijing University, Mark Rowswell was invited to take part in a stage performance playing the role of a Chinese young man named Xu Dashan. His fluent Chinese, naughty words and the use of Chinese slang frequently made the audience laugh. As a result, the name of "Dashan" stuck. Dashan's Chinese-speaking abilities were further enhanced when he decided to become a student of a well-known cross-talk performer. Cross-talk, one of the linguistic performing arts deeply loved by the Chinese people, has a rich folk culture. The experience of learning the cross-talk patter not only enabled Dashan to master the multiple ways of expressing himself in Chinese, but also gave him insights into the life of ordinary Chinese and their way of thinking. As Dashan has said, he has been taking cross-talk as a window to know all aspects of China.

After graduating from Beijing University, Dashan worked in the cultural section of the Canadian Embassy in China for three years. During this period, he developed some new ideas on cross cultural exchange. He said that foreigners did not understand the Chinese and vice versa. In fact, this was an ideological difference. He felt that merely conducting some food festivals could not enhance the friendship between the Canadian and Chinese peoples nor produce any depth in understanding. In 1995, Dashan left the embassy and registered a Dashan Company Ltd. in Canada, aiming at introducing Canada to the Chinese people and vice versa.

Dashan's company cooperated with the Canadian National Film Office and shot a film introducing China in the 1990s. The film was well received. In 2003, his Chinese teaching program for foreigners was broadcast by CCTV international channel. In China, Dashan is often involved in commercial activities and public welfare undertakings. Sometimes, he also gives cross-talk shows. "China's ordinary people bestowed this name Dashan on me and regard me as a friend and even as 'one of them'. So, I should try my best to do some beneficial things to enhance the understanding between China and the West," he said.

Dashan's Chinese wife and two children now live in Canada. Every year, Dashan stays in China for half a year and spends the other half in Canada. He said, "I am an ordinary foreigner and I like to live an ordinary person's life, coming to China happily and returning to Canada safely."

↑ Reading books in Beijing University.
← Chinese audiences' favorite foreign comic star Dashan.

22

With cross-talk master Hou Baolin.

"I must let my son study Chinese culture well, from his childhood."

Learning to cook Chinese dishes is one of his hobbies.

Performing with his beloved tutor Ding Guangquan.
Dashan in a Peking Opera costume.

Jenny and Jessie with Their Chinese Parents

○ Photos by Wang Jie

Jenny and Jessie, who come from California, lived with a three-member family in Shanghai with the help of the Shanghai Municipal Government Foreign Affairs Office and the Caoyang community of Putuo District. The experience allowed them to share in the life of an ordinary Shanghai family.

In recent years, the number of foreign students coming to study in China has been increasing. They either come to receive a Chinese education in universities or have short-term training and cultural exchanges. It is common to see the exchanges among middle school students enabling them to live in each other's host families. Jenny and Jessie are very happy to become "host daughters" of a Shanghai family.

Jenny and Jessie's Chinese father is very kind and their mother is good at singing and dancing. Their Chinese sister is studying in middle school. During the daytime, the two American sisters study Chinese at the East China Normal University. For the first few days, the host parents and their children had to communicate with hand gestures to express their meaning. One time, the Chinese father wanted to tell Jenny she could take a shower, but had forgotten the English word "shower". Then the father made a gesture to show the action of scrubbing his back. Jenny misunderstood and thought the father wanted her to go dancing. She put on her clothes and was ready to go. At last, the whole family laughed.

Every morning, Jenny and Jessie go to a farm produce market with their Chinese mother. They bargain with the Chinese vegetable growers and meat sellers with both gestures and some Chinese. Some sellers give in to the foreign girl's bargaining powers and offer them a price lower than the market price. After that, Jessie goes with the mother to the park to learn *mulanquan* boxing, a kind of martial art like *taijiquan*, which is suitable for women. Jessie said she must master it so as to be able to open a *mulanquan* martial art class after returning to the United States. At the weekend, the two American sisters go sightseeing with their Chinese parents and tour the Nanjing Road, China's "Manhattan". Seeing the crowded streets, the two girls were surprised and said they had seen more people in a day in Shanghai than in a week in California!

A month passed quickly and in the Chinese family Jenny and Jessie personally experienced the Chinese people's kindness and hospitality. Their Chinese parents know that the American children's achievements are worth praising. The girls have improved their oral Chinese and could cook several Chinese dishes. Jessie also mastered *mulanquan* boxing skills.

↗ Jenny learns how to cook Chinese dishes and affectionately kisses her Chinese father.
→ Jessie dances to the sounds of Karaoke music.

↑ "We love Chinese *jiaozi* (dumplings)."
→ Jessie practices *mulanquan* boxing.

↑ Jenny often argues with her Chinese sister.
↖ *Mahjong* attracts the American girls.
← American girl enters a Chinese kitchen.

Writer Lisa Carducci

Photos by Wang Qifa

Lisa Carducci has Italian origin but actually comes from Canada. A writer and language expert, she is fluent in French and Italian, and can speak English and Chinese, as well as Spanish. Lisa, who was a teacher in Canada, worked as a teacher in China for two years, then engaged in French polishing, editing and dubbing work in CCTV for six years. Since 1999 until now, she has been working as a French expert at *Beijing Review* under the China Foreign Languages Publishing and Distribution Administration. Though always very busy, Lisa likes the work.

When she first came to China, Lisa often felt the cultural differences. She said, "China is unique indeed. If I always remain in the past mode of thinking, then this will collide with the reality. I have to get rid of my original thinking, affections, beliefs, and even culture, to objectively observe China with new eyes." Living in Beijing for a dozen years, Lisa has changed her views of China a great deal. She said people who sleep on three-wheel carts or under the shadow of trees at noon are not homeless people as sometimes imagined by foreigners. In China, taking a break after lunch is people's custom and is natural. She has witnessed many changes in Beijing. Fifteen years ago, there were few taxis cabs on the streets, but now they are countless. The Internet was not known several years ago, but now Lisa's Chinese friends all have their own e-mail address.

Lisa has financed seven poverty-stricken children to go to school through "Project Hope". She said: "Project Hope is a public welfare undertaking relying on goodwill and generous people to support poor children to go to school." So, she is all for it. Lisa hopes that more foreigners can understand the efforts made by the Chinese people for the development of their country. She has written thousands of articles published by both Chinese and foreign newspapers and magazines. Among the 30 or so books she has written in French, Italian and English, half are related to China. Lisa has also seen China's problems. For example, while many people are dedicating themselves to the country's development and prosperity with their pure Communist spirit, others have become corrupt and have damaged the public interests for their own personal gain. She does not know how to solve this problem.

Lisa's husband is a Chinese artist. Lisa is also keen on painting and has held two painting exhibitions in Beijing, donating all the income from them to the Project Hope. Lisa has done many social beneficial works. She is a volunteer for Beijing environmental protection and has donated blood 22 times without any pay. So, many Chinese people honored her as "Doctor Bethune the Second." But Lisa said, "Even though many people call me 'Laowai' (old foreigner), I am not used to the name. In fact, I will never be. I love China like all of you and will continue to live here."

In 2001, Lisa was granted the "Friendship Award" by the State Bureau of Foreign Experts Affairs.

↑ "Me, cover girl? Don't kid me!"
→ Look, I am the person behind Pu Cunxi !
(photo by Yvonne Gluyas)

↑ Lisa likes to show Beijing to her visiting family
members. (photo by Olga Cassetta)

Singing Christmas songs at the Friendship Hotel.
"Writing means a rest to me," said Lisa.
At Zhenbeitai of the Great Wall in Shaanxi
Province with her husband. (photo by Xie Feng)

↑ Lisa's home is full of Chinese folk art products.
↖ Crossing a river in Yunnan Province with members
  of the Naxi nationality. (photo by Du Jinsu)
↖ One, two, three, go. (photo by Du Jinsu)

Back to Home from America

Photos by Xin Yongjun

"I really cannot believe this is true!" said the 71-year-old Joseph who arrived at Jinan Railway Station in Shandong Province with his wife on the No. K35 train. He is as excited as a child.

Joseph's father, a Swede, came to Shandong Province as a missionary in 1925. He met an American nurse in Qingdao Hospital and they married. In 1927, Joseph Snr. accompanied his wife to the United States, where she gave birth to the Joseph Jnr. In 1928, the child came to Shandong with his parents and spent an unforgotten childhood in a village named Longshan until 1936.

Now, Joseph Jnr. is in his 70s and living in the United States. But he always recalled his past while living in China. Several years ago, he sent an E-mail to Shandong's Qilu Evening News, asking for help to find his childhood place. With some difficulty, a reporter found the village in Zhangqiu City where Joseph once lived, and to which he soon returned.

Seeing the enthusiastic and cordial villagers who came to greet him, Joseph was soon in tears. The houses and cypress trees brought back memories of his childhood years. The house built by his father is still there, and the scenes when he and other children went to a railway station by bike and played together, passed before his eyes. An 81-year-old villager tightly held Joseph's hand and asked him in broken English: "Do you still remember me? Your father once taught me English and came to my home." Joseph sobbed and recalled the scene when he and his little friend once studied English together under an old tree more than 60 years ago.

Joseph and his wife stayed in Longshan for two days. The local government and the villagers embraced this American "relative" with honest and warm affection. The villagers treated Joseph and his wife as their own loved ones and invited them to their homes, talking and chatting cordially. Other villagers gave Joseph tobacco that he liked. The strong affection of the folks drove away Joseph's bitterness of the long absence and warmed his heart. Under the old cypress tree, he took out a small bottle full of earth that he brought from the United States and carefully spread it under the tree. "Today, I spread the earth here. Hereafter, the home in Longshan and the home in the United States will be connected forever." Joseph said: "In affection, I am neither a native of Sweden nor an American, but I am from Longshan of China. My roots are in China and after my death half of my ashes will be buried in Longshan."

When the couple left the village, the Longshan Township Government presented Joseph with a certificate of an "Honorary Villager of Longshan Town in Zhangqiu City". Joseph said happily: "This is the highest honor in my life." He expressed a plan to make the certificate into a copper plate and hang it in his American house.

← "I am coming back to my hometown!"

FOREIGNERS IN CHINA

FOREIGNERS IN CHINA

↑ The old home's pipe tobacco is Joseph's favorite.
↗ Delicious Longshan millet gruel.
⇢ It is very hard to find the tracks of the old days in
the Longshan streets.

⇡ Returning to his old home, Joseph cannot stop the tears coming into his eyes.
⇡ Childhood partners.
⇢ Spreading a bottle of earth brought from the United States, so that the home in Longshan and the home in the United State will be connected forever.

Yiwu Is My Home

© Photos by Dai Shulin

Harid, like many Chinese fathers, wakes up his son every morning. Finishing their breakfast in a hurry, Harid sends his son to school and then goes off to work.

Harid is a Pakistani businessman. He first set up a company in Xinjiang Uygur Autonomous Region in 1987, but the business did not go well. In 1993, Harid made an inspection tour in Yiwu, Zhejiang Province. Yiwu is a city known for its small commodities of numerous varieties and low prices, attracting many business people from home and abroad. Established in 1982, the China Small Commodities City in Yiwu seemed the ideal base for Harid's business.

Harid rents several rooms in the Honglou Hotel near the small commodity city and engages in selling stationary, arts and crafts, as well as toys. One time, he purchased more than 200 slicing knives and found that every box was missing one knife. He was very worried about it. His Chinese friend reported the matter to the market's industrial and commercial office. "I didn't expect the department would attach much importance to it. But, they immediately found the seller and made up the deficiency. The industrial and commercial department also apologized to me on behalf of the seller," said Harid. This matter enhanced his confidence to do business in Yiwu.

The prosperous market has attracted many business people from Pakistan, the Arabian region, Nepal, Jordan, and Russia. In October 2000, Harid rented space on the second floor of the Honglou Hotel and opened a restaurant offering authentic Muslim food. He invited his brother to be the manager and also invited three chefs from Pakistan. Arabian business people now often hold a party and exchange information in this restaurant.

Currently, more than 3,800 foreign business people in over 300 foreign companies permanently reside in Yiwu to engage in small commodity business. Harid, a chief representative of a Pakistan enterprise, is now selling radios, tape recorders and cameras to the Middle East and other parts of the world. He and his Chinese wife, Xie Mingxia, have two lovely children, a son and a daughter. Harid said: "I like the life here and Yiwu is my own home."

↗ Love across the boundary has borne sweet fruit — two lovely children.
↦ On the way back from the kindergarten, Harid drops in on roadside shops to learn the market situation.

46

↑ Harid talks with his customers in fluent Chinese.
↖ Harid establishes goodwill relations with many local businesses.
← It is a pleasure for Harid to host friends from his hometown.

Serving the People

Photos by Zhang Zhiping

There is a Xiangyang District in Xiangfan City, Hubei Province. There is also a Xiangyang Prefecture in the Republic of Korea (ROK). In 1997, China's Xiangyang District and ROK's Xiangyang Prefecture became sister cities. In September 2001, the two local governments decided on an exchange program of their officials for a year, so as to broaden their experiences in administrative management. On February 25, 2002, the ROK side sent a woman named Nam to China to act as assistant of the director of Xiangyang District Government Office.

"Xiangyang is my home and I am one of them," wrote Nan Meiai, on the day she arrived. She never expected that her new colleagues would treat her so warmly. It was China's Spring Festival when she first came to Xiangyang. From the first to the fourth day of the New Year, she received invitations from 10 families that helped her overcome any feelings of homesickness.

However, Nam was very strict in her work. She found that some people often came late and others went from office to office chatting during working hours. In her far-from-fluent Chinese, she made suggestions to the office director and said, "the staff members here are not disciplined." The director adopted her suggestions, calling for all departments to strictly implement office rules and regulations. The director also criticized these people.

There are great differences between the two countries in civil servants' way of working and work content, which Nan was not used to. However, she has found a common objective—serving the people. One day, she saw a slogan on a street wall: "Serve the People Wholeheartedly". She immediately jumped off her bus and took a picture, saying, "The requirements for civil servants in each country are almost the same."

Nam has never lost a chance to serve the people. From a newspaper, she learnt about a "volunteer team" in Xiangfan that regularly helps residents in difficulties. She then contacted them and went with them to do volunteer work. During the May Day holiday, she took part in a festival party held by Xiangfan Peking Opera Troupe. Little performers greeted her in Korean and hoped she would teach them her language. Thereafter, she went to the opera troupe to teach them Korean every weekend. She also taught the district's government officials and staff members. Through studying Korean, her Xiangyang townsmen gained a strong interest in Korean customs and local flavors. She said, "Teaching Korean also means to serve the people!"

Through a year's work in Xiangyang, she has become a friendship bridge connecting the two cities. She established her own website, introducing Xiangfan's culture and development. After reading this, many Korean people left messages for her in the hope that they could learn more about Xiangfan and expressed an interest in traveling there.

↑ On the invitation from the Xiangfan District People's Government, Nam becomes a civil servant of Xiangfan District Government.

↖ Making a business inspection tour in Chenghe Township, Xiangfan District.

← Whenever she has time, Nam goes to help families in difficulties with their household chores.

↑ Attending the district's people's congress.

↑ Nam sometimes argues with her Chinese friends due to different views on values.

↑ Nam often goes to the Korean restaurant in Xiangfan street.

↑ Inspecting the Hanjiang River with Chinese colleagues,
Nam feels like she is back in her hometown.
⇢ She loves all aspects of life.

Children at the International School

The rapid economic development in Hangzhou of Zhejiang Province has attracted many foreign investors. In 2002, the number of foreign-funded enterprises and Sino-foreign joint ventures in the city exceeded 1,700. Permanently living in the city, these foreign investors brought their families with them and their children needed education. Because of the language barrier and the difference in the educational systems of China and other countries, many parents hoped their children could enjoy a Western education here. In the past, there was no international school in Hangzhou, so they had to send their children to the Shanghai International School, which is 300 km away.

Therefore, the Hangzhou City government decided to open an international school in its own high-tech industrial development zone, with the school site provided by the Hangzhou Educational Bureau. It is set up and managed by the International School Development of America (ISDA), which has opened many international schools around the world, in such places as Indonesia, South Africa and China.

The Hangzhou International School is the seventh school established by ISDA. The first batch of students are those living in Hangzhou and the surrounding areas, with their parents who come from abroad or from Hong Kong, Macao and Taiwan.

The American dean, Derek invited some foreign professional teachers who come from the United States, Britain, New Zealand and Indonesia to join him. The school adopts American teaching methods, which are very suitable to these foreign children who had studied in their home country and will go back eventually to continue their study there. Currently, the foreign teachers and their multi-national students are happy in the school.

↑ "I am excellent!" Dylan is very confident in doing everything.
→ A foreign teacher vividly tells a story to the children.

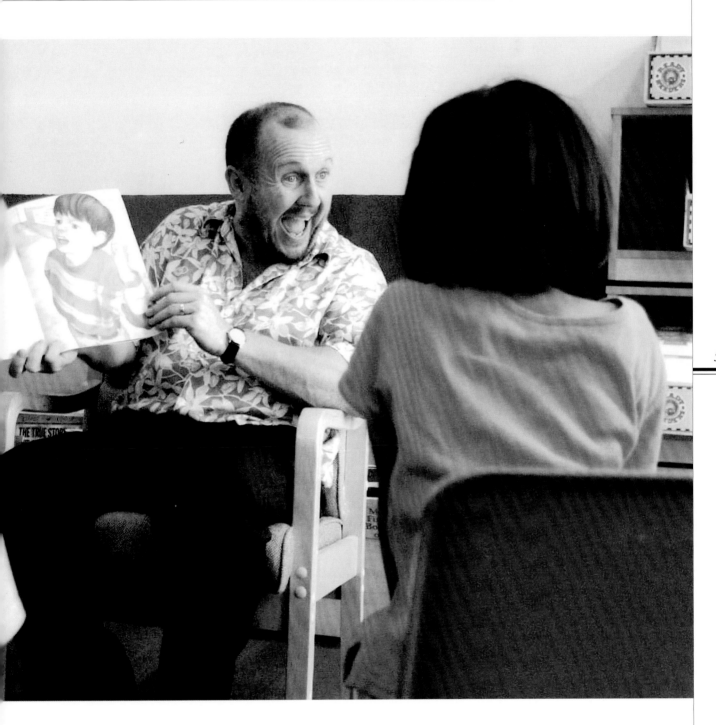

➢ Naughty boy students are careless when doing their homework.

➢ I still like to have milk and bread.

➢ Eliot likes the music class.

➢ Expressing happiness, this student mirrors his teacher.

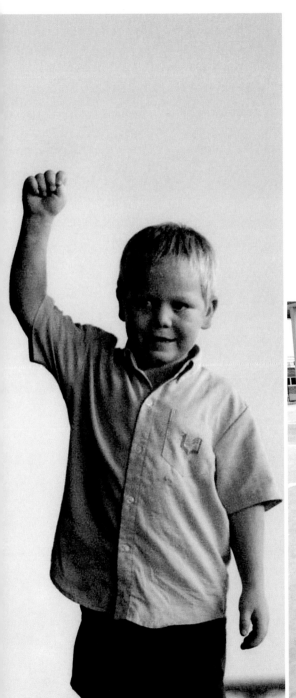

← Happy time.
↓ Facing the huge basketball, this little boy seems to lose his confidence.

FOREIGNERS IN CHINA

"Foreign Foremen" at the Three Gorges Worksite

◎ Photos by Sun Ronggang

At the worksite of the Three Gorges Water Conservancy Project, there are more than 20 "foreign foremen" coming from the United States, Britain, France, Germany, Japan and Switzerland. They are in charge of technical guidance for the Three Gorges dams' cement pouring, installation of generators and construction safety. Together with the Chinese constructors, they are busy and working hard for the Three Gorges Project. Noff, a native of Switzerland, is one of them.

Coming to China in 1998, he took part in the construction of the Guigang Water Conservancy Project in Guangxi Zhuang Autonomous Region and the Foshan Water Conservancy Project in Guangdong Province. In April 2002, the 34-year-old Swiss technician came to work for the Three Gorges Project, helping with installation of the generators.

The Three Gorges Water Conservancy Project is the world's biggest construction project. Started in 1992, it is expected to be completed in 2009. The Swiss technician arrived at the worksite during construction of the second-phase project. During this period, construction of power facilities and the installation of 14 generators must be completed in the left side dam. The Swiss technician worked conscientiously and took everything very seriously, winning praise from his Chinese colleagues. Sometime, he is "too stubborn" to be accepted. But he said: "We must work in accordance with the rules, and cannot give up our principles." He likes the work and feels proud to be participating in such a world-famous project. He is also proud of his family because he married a Chinese woman named He Xiaojun when he worked on the Guigang Water Conservancy Project. While installing the equipment, he is also building his own home of love.

← Guiding workers to prepare for welding work.

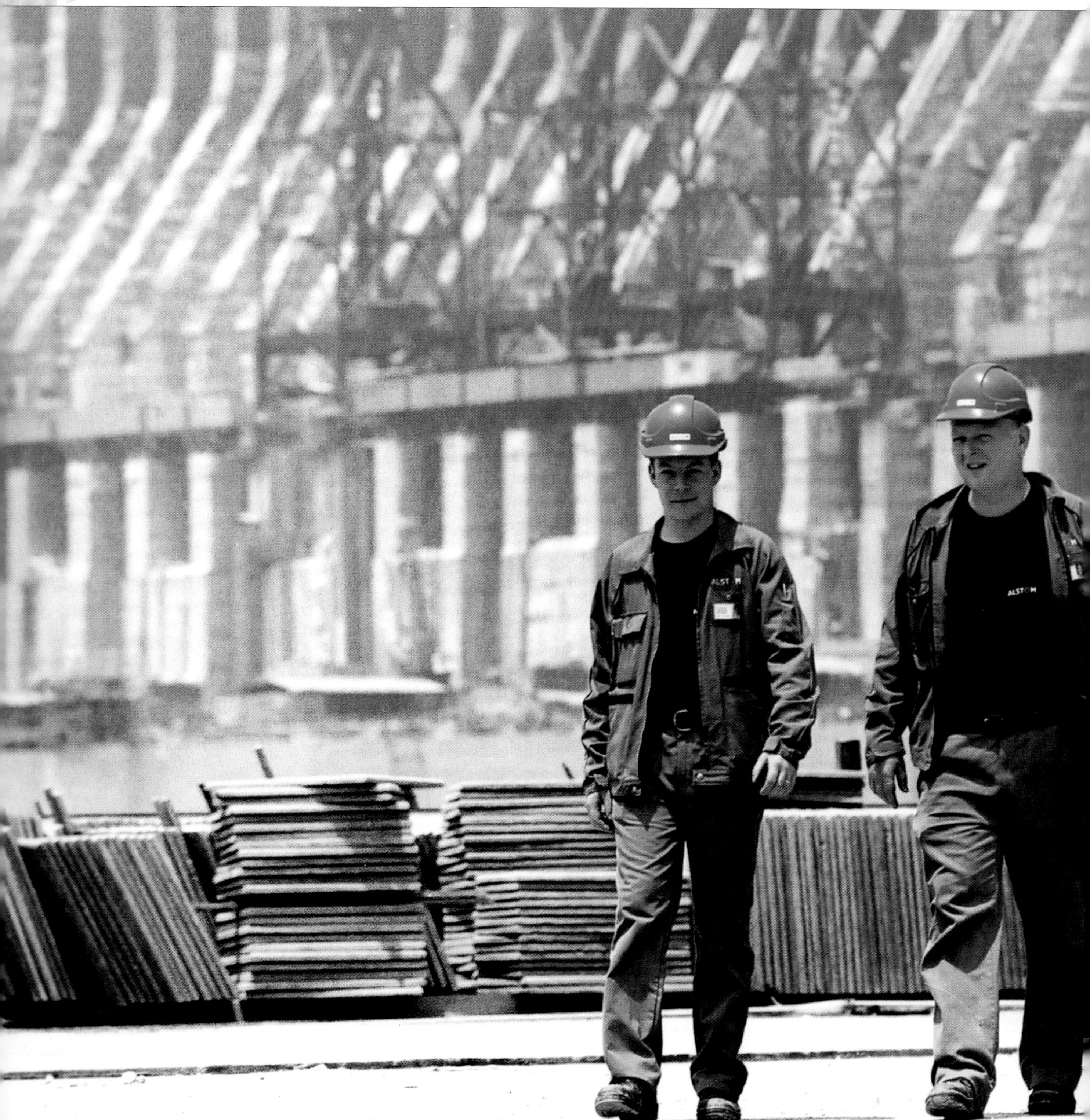
ALSTOM

↑ With their marriage certificate, the couple live a happy life filled with love.
← Walking with colleagues.

The Swiss technician and his colleagues form ties of deep
affection in China.
Testing the generators of the Three Gorges Project.

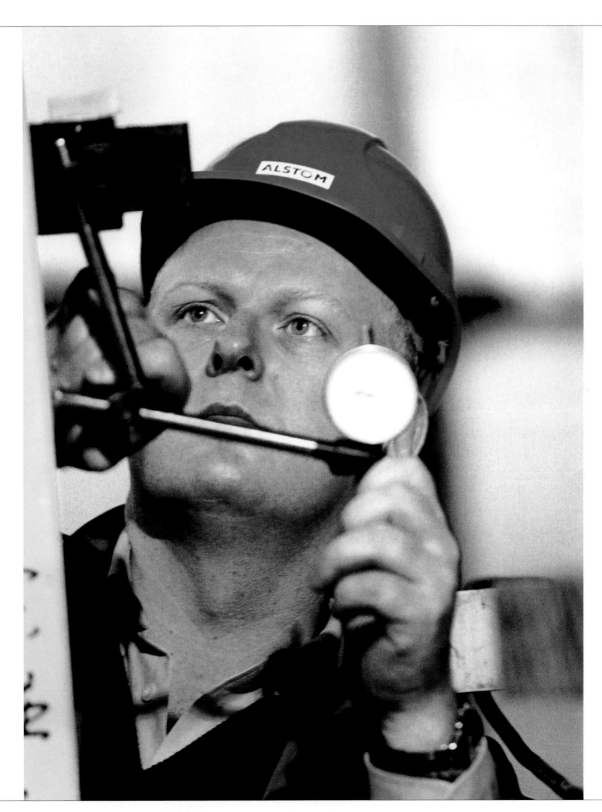

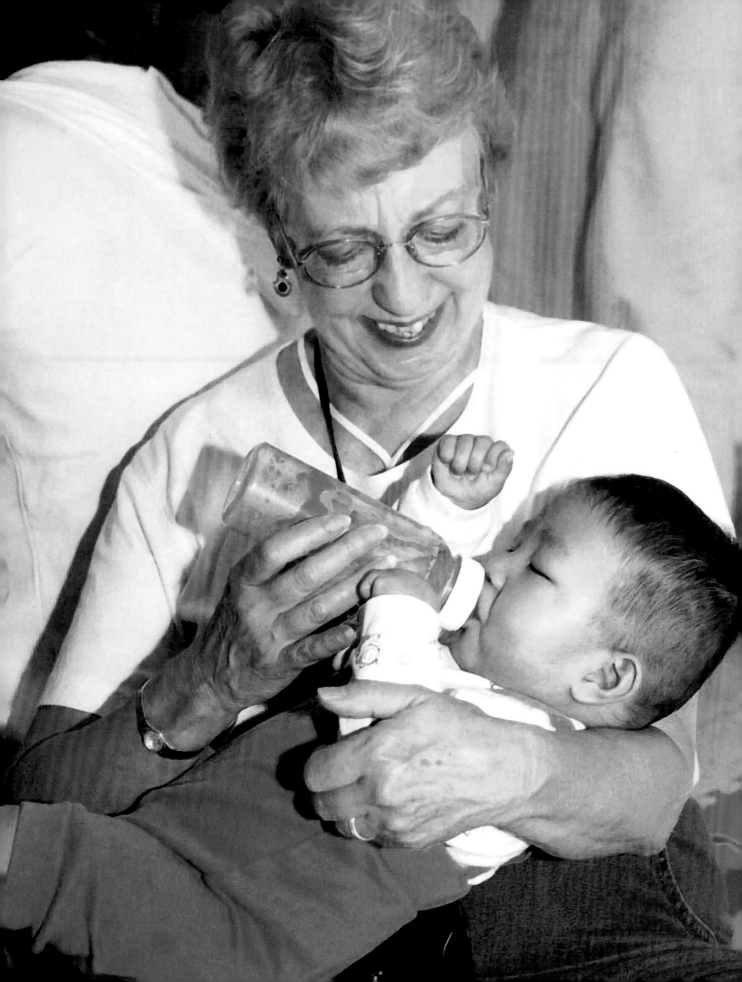

Kind Ambassador

○ Photos by Zhang Guanghui

In June 2002, 37 American volunteers came to work for a week in the Luoyang Children Welfare Center in Henan Province. The volunteers came from the U.S-China Adoption Federation, the U. S. Phillip Heide Fund and the U.S. CBN Company. For most it was their first visit to China.

The Luoyang Children Welfare Center is a social welfare institution that adopts orphans and disabled children. One year ago, the New York Times carried an article introducing the center. Thereafter, many American people got to know that there were a group of orphans and disabled children in China who needed to be taken care of. Volunteers of the U.S.-China Adoption Federation and other charity organizations expressed a desire to go to China to help. On June 2, 2002, 37 volunteers set out for China with help from the China Youth Travel Service.

After arriving at the welfare center, the volunteers were divided into several teams. Some of them helped the disabled children to conduct rehabilitation training, some of them taught the children English, others played games with them, and still others looked after infants. They bought the best quality environmentally friendly paint and detergents for the desks, chairs and restrooms. Jeannette, a diplomat, was doubled over, carefully painting the desks and chairs. After a whole day's work, her clothes were covered with paint and her hands were stiff. But the next day, she was back at work on time.

Despite difficulties in communicating, the volunteers patiently taught the children to play games. In order to save time and do more for the children, they did not go to their hotel for lunch. They donated money and bought clothes, toys, medicines and air conditioners for the children. As most of them came to China for the first time, the related department had especially arranged a proper travel program, but they gently refused. They said, "Thank you for your kindness but we are coming to do volunteer work, not for touring." However, they were delighted to bring the children to visit parks in Luoyang. Carrying infants in their arms and leading the older children by the hand, the volunteers treated the children as if they were their own.

↗ Starting the train game.
← A volunteer takes time to feed one of many orphans.

↑ Like a real mother and son.
↖ Manager of the New York Computer Training Center is
teaching the children to speak English.
← Jeannette carefully painting the desks.

↑ Registered nurse Joyce Gilliam guiding the disabled children in rehabilitation training.

↑ Children are happy to see the colorful bubbles under the sun.

↖ Enjoying the sunshine while walking in the city.

A Family in Chongqing

Photos by Ran Wen

John Sebastian gave his Chinese-born son a chinese name—Lei Feng. A soldier who died on duty in the 1960s, Lei Feng is a household hero in China, and his spirit of "serving the people wholeheartedly" has been praised by and has deeply influenced the Chinese people. The "Lei Feng" in John Sebastian's family is now aged four so his life has only just begun.

"The Chinese people stress family, affection and friendship, which is very beneficial to children's growth," said Sebastian.

This 48-year-old American now teaches English and business at the Chongqing University's Foreign Languages Institute. Chongqing, located in southwestern China, is a beautiful mountain city. John and his wife like this city. They live in an old-style building near the institute. Beside two daughters in the United States, five younger children all live with them. Gina, John's wife, does not work but shoulders the heavy duty of educating the children.

"We help our children find their interests and then support them," said John. The eight-year-old son is keen on study, particularly history. Gina is in charge of his study and they have finished the course of world history. Though studying at home, Gina takes the course seriously. Their 13-year-old daughter has broad interests and she likes Chinese martial arts and painting, studying Chinese and playing table tennis. John hired three Chinese teachers for her. Their 15-year-old daughter, is a pretty girl and likes to make up every time when going out. She is now taking a computer course. She also likes to cook Chinese food with her mother. The 19-year-old son moves around likes the wind, and his mother never knows where he is and when he will come home. He is now studying Chinese and preparing to enter Chongqing University's Film and Television Institute in the hope of becoming a movie star.

The couple works hard to arrange their home in Chinese style. Chinese calligraphy and paintings hang on the walls. Copies of ceramic works of the Ming and Qing dynasties sit on a Chinese style cupboard. In the corner of the room is an old-style wooden chopping block, on which an iron bowl has been placed. The furniture in the living room is old Chinese furniture bought from a second-hand market. John only spent 80 yuan on a bed carved with flower patterns. After being painted by Gina and the two daughters, it became very beautiful.

Sebastian and his family have lived in China for six years. He said, "If it is possible, I will continue to live here. I like Chongqing. I love China."

↑ Gina teaches the youngest son to build with wood.
↖ The happy faces of the Sebastian family.

↑ Learning Chinese *Kongfu* with his fourth daughter.
↗ When busy with work, they buy Chinese fast food in the street.
→ John bargains with street peddlers.

↑ The third daughter can also help with
household chores.
↑ Gina lies on the bed tutoring the children.
⇢ Every day, John and his wife go for a walk
with their children.

Madam Ambassador

Photos by Liang Zhijun

Two rooms of the Japanese ambassador's residence in Beijing are covered in artifacts and photographs depicting China's history of Buddhism. They are the proud collection of Anami Fumiyo, wife of the Japanese Ambassador, and a keen Chinese historian and photographer, who has painstakingly classified her anthology in accordance with the history of Liao (916-1125) and Jin (1115-1234) dynasties and Buddhist history. For Anami Fumiyo, this collection has become an inseparable part of her life.

An American-born naturalized Japanese citizen, Anami Fumiyo, a scholar studying Chinese history, most notably the history of Buddhism in China, developed her interest in these subjects from her father. Growing up under the influence of her father who was working in the Far East, Anami Fumiyo (Virginia Helen Stibbs) studied the history of China and the history of Buddhism. In 1967, she came to study Chinese in Taiwan where she met a young Japanese diplomat Anami Koreshige. Three years later, she became his wife.

During her time in Beijing, she has widely researched China's Liao and Jin dynasties, discovering that the two dynasties had established their capital in Beijing and constructed several temples. Sadly, today only an ancient tree and tablet are all that is left of that time. Guided by the directions of an old map, Anami has found 350 Buddhist sites surrounding Beijing, recording and photographing the locations and cultural relics of these temples, while noting the many legends handed down by local people. Her work has aroused great interest from Chinese historians, who invited her to take part in the seminar commemorating the 850 years of anniversary of the establishment of Beijing. She has also held eight solo exhibitions in both Beijing and Japan.

Fumiyo said she respects Japanese monk Enjin who traveled to China in the ninth century to study Buddhism. Following in the tracks of Enjin and visiting all the sites that Enjin had left, she believes the monk was not only a Buddhist believer, but also a religious and cultural envoy. Now Fumiyo is doing just what Enjin did, converting the history of classics into vivid and interesting stories to attract more people. This has led her to make many Chinese friends, including those experts studying the history of the Liao and Jin dynasties, as well as the elderly living near the sites, who told her long forgotten stories about the temples. Fumiyo believes her contact with all these people has improved her own life as well as playing an important role in her diplomatic work.

↑ Yinshan Talin in Changping District, a pagoda built in the Jin Dynasty still standing in the Yinshan Mountain. (photo by Anami Fumiyo)
← The wife of the ambassador. (photo by Huang Xu)

FOREIGNERS IN CHINA

↑ Anami Fumiyo pays a visit to the abbot Fayu in the Lingjing Temple, located in Lingjing Village, south of the Wutaishan Mountain in Shanxi Province.

↖ Photo exhibition on Beijing's Liao and Jin cultures, held by Anami Fumiyo in Xin Dongan Market in October 2002.

↙ Dingcun villagers in Shanxi Province welcome Fumiyo and other foreign friends. (photo by Liu Xiaodao)

⬆ Fumiyo and her husband Anami Koreshige.

⬈ Fumiyo practices *taijiquan* in the ambassador's residence of the Japanese Embassy. She has studied Chinese *kongfu* for 36 years. (photo by Huang Xu)

↑ Family photo taken in 2001 in the Beijing Zoo. They also had a
family photo taken in the same place 26 years before.

Foreign Models in Beijing

Photos by Lu Beifeng

Forty-nine supermodels from all parts of the world gathered at the banquet hall of the Sheraton Great Wall Hotel Beijing, showing off different colors of beauty in their Chinese surroundings. These models came to China to take part in the final competition of the Ford Supermodels of the World.

International fashion has recently been eyeing China after discovering that there were not only numerous girls longing to be models, but also many commercial opportunities. The Ford Models Inc., which discovered many world famous models and film stars, including Sharon Stone, Brooke Shields and Jane Fonda, decided to stage the final competition in Beijing. Coming to Beijing from various parts of the world, these beautiful models add the international flavor to this famous oriental city.

As it was their first trip to Beijing, the models only knew China from magazines and TV programs. For them, China was a remote and wonderful dream destination. But when they came to this land of ancient and modern civilization, seeing the magnificent Great Wall, the solemn and splendid Tiananmen Square and the sumptuous Palace Museum, they felt their dream had been realized. While in Beijing, they personally flew a kite, wrote their names in Chinese with calligraphy brushes and learnt how to use chopsticks. In addition, the mysteries of Chinese chess and the charm of the panda all made a deep impression on them. One model could not help saying: "Beijing is very beautiful, China is very beautiful."

They have really enjoyed China's unique oriental culture and tasted its flavors. China has also enjoyed the charm of the world's top models.

"I want to fly a kite."
→ Visiting the Forbidden City.

← Foreign models and the "old Beijing" at the Huangchenggen Site.

↑ Playing with a Seal.
← China's panda toys become their favorite souvenirs.

← Using chopsticks for the
first time.
→ "We have climbed the
Great Wall."

Affection for the Sea

◎Photos by Yang Jichen

In the beautiful coastal city of Weihai, on November 21, 2000, an English bridegroom wearing formal dress and hat, and shouldering a piece of red silk, slowly lifted the red square piece of silk that covered the head of his Chinese bride. This, in accordance with the traditional Chinese customs, symbolizes that the girl now belonged to him.

The bridegroom, Nigel, is a native of Leeds in England. He is the only boy in the family. His father has a high social status and is well off, so that Nigel enjoyed a good life in Britain. However, he did not want to remain at home but flew to China to develop his own life.

Just as the Chinese saying goes: "It must be fate that people are brought together from thousands of miles away." Nigel happened to meet the Chinese girl Li Jing in Beijing. Li is a native of Weihai City in Shandong Province. Several years ago, she was enrolled in Beijing Commercial University majoring in foreign trade in English. She found a job in Beijing after graduating. When Nigel came to China from Britain, the two met at Beijing Airport and loved each other at first sight.

Growing up in a traditional Chinese family, Li Jing takes her marriage very seriously. She kept her thoughts about Nigel to herself and responded to Nigel's straightforwardness with the Chinese way of implicitness. When he proposed to her, the girl was not sure, and silently left Beijing and lived in her sister's home in Weihai.

Nigel, however, did not give up. He worked very hard and was determined to prove his capabilities by the success of his undertaking, and at the same time, he kept in touch with Li Jing. Every weekend, Nigel came to Weihai to see her. Half a year later, the Chinese girl was conquered by the real affection and love he showed. Upon approval by her parents, Li Jing went with Nigel to Britain. Nigel's parents are also very careful with the son's marriage. The father flew to Weihai to visit Li Jing's family members. He saw with his own eyes Weihai's beautiful and natural environment and fine climate. He also liked the family members' honesty and kindness. Therefore, he and Li Jing's parents discussed and arranged the wedding.

In late autumn, the wedding ceremony was held in Weihai, and Nigel's mother and sisters came from Britain to take part. The bride and bridegroom selected China's traditional wedding rites. Nigel finally lifted the red silk cover from the head of his bride. Now, they have a daughter and Nigel's parents have become foreign relatives of Weihai.

↑ Raising the red head cover in their bridal chamber.
↗ The loving couple finally become husband and wife.
⇒ The couple's parents wish their children a happy life.

↑ A year later, the young couple has a daughter
named Li Baobao.
→ Back from a trip.

Woman Host in a Mountain Inn

© Photos by Jing Guangping

The enchanting natural scenery of the Hutiaoxia Gorge located in Yunnan Province attracted Margaret, an Australian woman then studying Chinese in Yunnan University, when she visited the place with her schoolmates in October 1996. She thought she would be happy if she could live there all her life. When she entered an inn called Shanquan, it was just on suppertime. The manager Xia Shanquan was preparing food for his clients, while his three little daughters played in the courtyard, where Margaret soon joined them.

Though the scenery of the Hutiaoxia Gorge is magnificent, communication links are inconvenient and the economy is backward. Accommodation is difficult for visitors to find. In the spring of 1987, Xia Shanquan, a young man who lived in Hetaoyuan Village of the Hutiaoxia Gorge, raised money and built a two-story building named Shanquan Inn, with 15 beds. Because most of the guests are foreigners, Xia became the first one to study English in the locality, and the guests were his teachers. He spent most of the time studying English and left all the household chores to his wife. But the wife could not bear the hard life with him and divorced him, leaving their three children with him. Thereafter, Xia had to take care of visitors and look after three youngsters. Moreover, the fact he had lost a hand in a fire made his life harder.

Deeply moved by Xia's honesty and strong will, Margaret got to love this kind and reliable young man. Returning to school, she wrote a letter to Xia, expressing her willingness: "I'd like to be the second boss of the Shanquan Inn." Xia thought Margaret was making a joke with him. On December the same year, Margaret came the second time to visit. Xia then believed what Margaret said in her letter was true. From then on, the two often contacted through letters pouring out their love for each other. In 1997, Xia Shanquan went to Australia and visited Margaret's family. Thereafter, they came back to the Hetaoyuan Village in Zhongdian County and married.

Every year, Margaret works in Australia for half a year and comes back to live in Hetaoyuan for the other half. She runs a small shop, and guides her husband to cook Western meals for foreign visitors. Margaret carefully takes care of the three children like a real mother. Lacking an easy material life does not change Margaret's love for Xia, but the hard life makes this Australian lady deeply love this land. Hetaoyuan has become her permanent living place.

With the expansion of the business, the number of beds in Shanquan has increased from 15 to 36. Every noon, Margaret writes down on a board the news she gets from radio broadcasts for visitors. As the economy is backward in the surrounding areas, in 1998, Zhongdian County built a highway leading to the Hutiaoxia Gorge instead of the former stone road, but travelers thought that the building of the road dimmed the natural scenery, and made it less attractive to foreign visitors, who declined in number. Missing those travelers on foot, the couple has a new plan to open up another route for walkers, hoping they will return to stay once more.

Every noon, Margaret offers visitors the latest news written on a board.

⇑ Margaret can use Chinese chopsticks.

⇑ Margaret becomes the English teacher of the three children after school.

⇐ Clean and comfortable Shanquan Inn attracts numerous Chinese and foreign customers.

FOREIGNERS IN CHINA

† Every evening, they stand in front of the
  gate to greet visitors.
→ Goodbye, my dear friend!

Bonnie and Beijing Hutongs

◎ Photos by Jiao Bo

American Bonnie Sayfer expected to come to Beijing again, after first visiting the capital in 1988. Bonnie is engaged in research on ancient architecture. When she stood in the center of Beijing, the Chinese capital with a history of 3,000 years, looking at the splendid Forbidden City and the surrounding hutongs (alleyways) stretching in all directions, as well as the traditional residential siheyuan (Beijing's courtyard house), she was stunned. In 1990, Bonnie and her husband moved to Beijing from Minnesota. Her husband worked at a foreign-funded enterprise and Bonnie taught American literature in the English Department of the Capital Normal University.

Beijing is marching towards being a modernized international city, with the old districts being transformed, so that the number of hutongs has been constantly reduced and many courtyard houses have disappeared to be replaced by skyscrapers. In order to keep the old Beijing style, the Beijing Municipal Government retained 25 residential areas of courtyard houses, renovating them and paving the streets in the hutongs, thus keeping the traditional architecture and flavor of old Beijing.

In her spare time, Bonnie likes to visit hutongs by bike, taking pictures and painting to record the time-honored lanes and courtyard houses, the gates with their stone sculptures and trees, as well as the elderly people who have long lived in the courtyards.

"Beijing's hutongs are the essence of traditional Chinese architecture," said Bonnie. In particular, she finds the gateways inside hutongs irresistible. Though the paint may have peeled off the pillars with the passing of time, they can still reveal something of the life inside. When she first came to Beijing, Bonnie only had the picture of closed gates taken, for fear of invading the hosts' "privacy." Later, an American friend who knew China well asked her: "Doesn't China's opening-up policy mean an open-door policy when being translated into English? You can therefore freely open the gates." Thereafter, Bonnie took many pictures of open gates and became good friends with a grandma living in one of the courtyards, dropping in for a chat every time she passed by.

Bonnie has been living in Beijing for a long time. When her friends praised her for her fluent oral Chinese, she modestly answered, "Mama Huhu" (just so-so.) While being praised for the pictures she took and paintings she drew, she still answered, "Mama Huhu". Then the friends said jokingly, "Do you still say mama huhu in regard to your affection of Beijing hutongs?" Bonnie answered quickly, "No! No!" She said it is very mysterious in the hutongs, and she might understand them even less when she leaves Beijing than when she first came here.

↑ Bonnie is surprised by Beijing architecture.
↖ Bonnie's sketch of a hutong.

↑ "Wait, let me sort out my clothes before my photo is taken."

↗ Wherever she goes, there is laughter. The hutong residents treat her as one of their own.

When coming back home, Bonnie's husband cooks
jiaozi (Chinese dumplings). Though the shape does
not look good, Bonnie praised the delicious taste.

Hutongs are full of flavor.

Taking amazing pictures.

Japanese Advisor Ryuzo Ozaki

◎ Photos by Gao Xingjian

When entering the Rirong Aquatic Food Co. Ltd. in Rizhao City, Shandong Province, you can see a slim elderly person busily moving about. He is Ryuzo Ozaki, a technology advisor of the Rirong Co., and well known in Japan's aquatic circles. Retiring in October 1997, he came to Rizhao City in Shandong Province at the invitation of the Rirong Aquatic Food Co. Ltd, to serve as a technological advisor.

The Rirong Aquatic Food Co. Ltd. is one of the key enterprises in Rizhao City and its products are well received in the Japanese market. Ryuzo had business contacts with the Rirong Company for more than a dozen years before he retired, and the two sides established good relations. He said, "I am willing to do something for the Rirong Company with my many years of experience." While acting as advisor, he came to the Rizhao City once or twice a month. Every time, he took away the aquatic samples to show to the Japanese market and brought back to China the Japanese market information and various ingredients for production. He said jokingly to the company's general manager, "I am shouldering three posts: I am not only your technological advisor, but also your head of transportation team, as well as your marketing manager."

With the help of the Japanese advisor, the Rirong Aquatic Food Co. Ltd. has established the mechanism and coordinated facilities for product development, experimentation and trial production. Its key product has been formed into more than 30 varieties in five series. In order to develop a new product, he has guided technicians to carry out experiments again and again. Some of the products have been selected after dozens of trials. The original leftover pieces are welcomed in Japanese market after being developed and promoted by Ryuzo. The Rirong Company has gained an increasing market share in Japan and has won more and more customers.

The Japanese advisor has offered great help to Rirong, but only asked for a low monthly salary from the company, which is only enough for his air ticket between China and Japan. During his work in Rizhao, he paid his own accommodation expenses. The company arranged for him many times to tour scenic spots and historical sites in the province, such as the Taishan Mountain and Qufu, but he gently refused. He said, "I have no other interest but my work."

↑ Working personally at the workshop.
↘ Writing down in detail technological data
   for the Rirong Company.

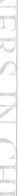

↑ Too busy to visit historical sites and scenic spots, he has to enjoy the scenery through the car window.

↑ Stressing high quality.

⇢ "I am your transportation team head."

⇢ Happily accepting the invitation letter from the Rirong Company.

Foreign Students at Beijing University

American former student Bailey really tasted Chinese-style kindness and warmth in Beijing University. When he first came to China, Bailey was always getting up late every morning, so his Chinese teacher began visiting his dormitory to wake him up. "It's time for class, Bailey. Please get up." He got his name through watching the Chinese opera Legend of the White Snake. At first, he named himself after one of the characters named Fahai, but his teachers were strongly opposed, because they did not like the negative role someone who suppressed the freedom of love. So, he had to change the name to Bailey.

Beijing University is one of the most prestigious universities in China since its founding at the end of the 19th Century. Its site is the campus of the former Yanjing University and people often call it "Yanyuan." Most of the foreign students who study there gain a deep impression of it, not only because of the good management and services they have enjoyed, but also due to the warmth and help they received from their Chinese teachers and classmates. Many students are reluctant to leave the school when they graduate.

After graduation, however, Bailey found a job in Beijing and was in charge of the Chinese business in the APCO Worldwide. He eats Chinese food, speaks Chinese and celebrates Chinese festivals. Beijing has become his "second home."

The education of foreign students at Beijing University started in 1952, with 14 coming from Eastern Europe. Now, it has more than 1,000 foreign students coming from over 70 countries, led by the Republic of Korea, Japan, the United States, Singapore, Indonesia and Britain. In 1997, Beijing University introduced entrance examinations for foreign students using tests it had designed. Except for English, all subjects must be answered in Chinese. Those who are enrolled through examinations study together with the Chinese students. Beijing University officials said that the purpose of the examination is to ensure the quality of the foreign students. Tangible results show that the subjects the foreign students selected are changing from the traditional archaeology, philosophy and Chinese language to finance, economy, astrophysics and other frontier subjects.

← Immortalising beautiful times at Beijing University.

← Happiness after completing the study.
↙ Great Chinese culture deeply attracts
overseas students.
↓ Studying for a Ph.D. in Biology, Mu, from
Congo, observes the growth of plants.

FOREIGNERS IN CHINA

↑ China's kites arouse great interest.
← Students listen to famous scholar Ji Xianlin.

↑ Celebrating Christmas.
↑ Foreign students' football team has taken part in Beijing competitions with good results.
→ Practicing Chinese Kung Fu in the early morning on campus.

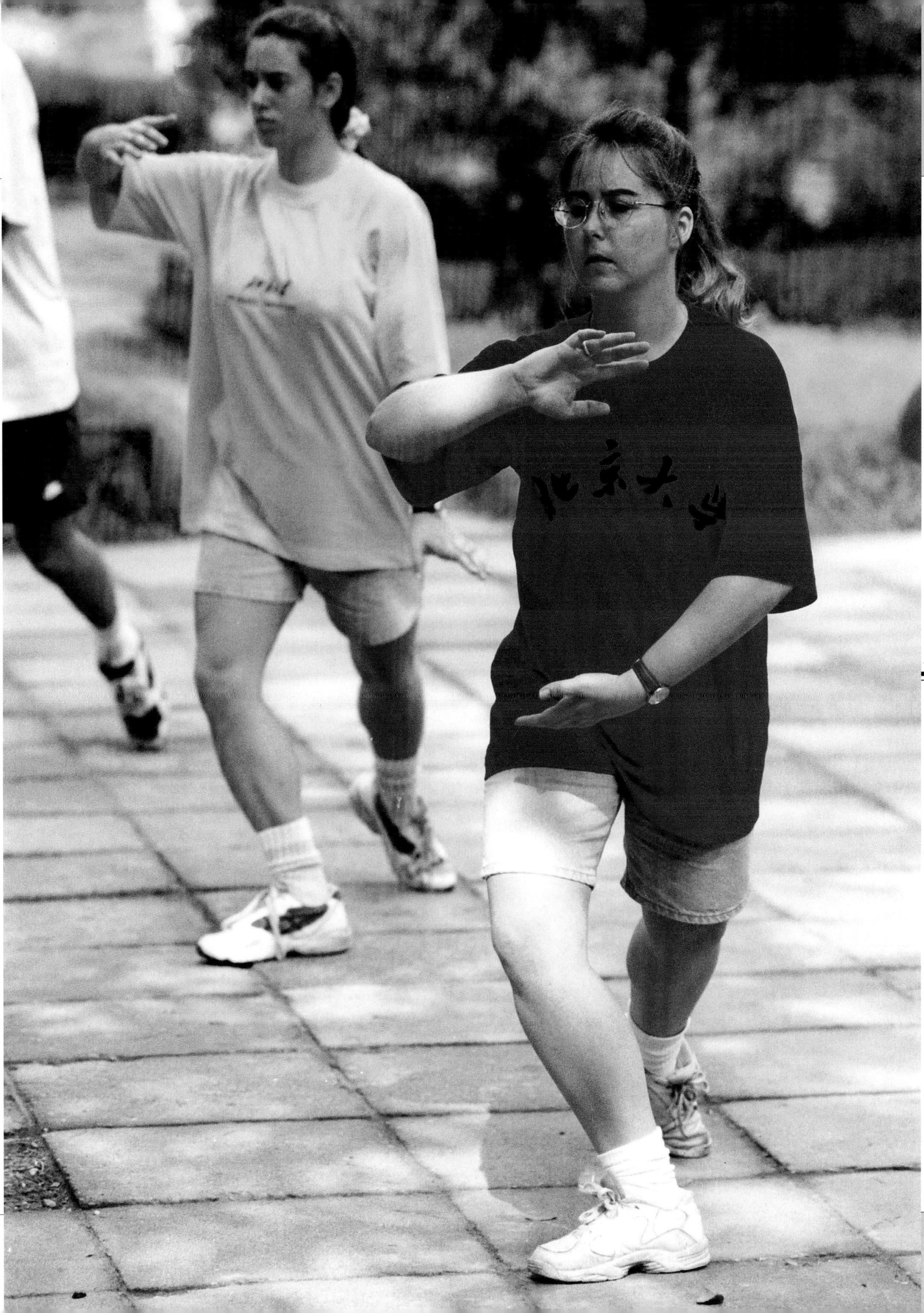
北京大学

Learning Chinese Martial Arts

◎ Photos by Wang Wenquan

Peter Reisman is the first American postgraduate studying in the Law Department of Beijing University. He came to China for two purposes: To study Chinese law and also to learn Chinese martial arts.

In August 1993, he began to study in Beijing University's martial arts class for foreign students. There, he met a good teacher, Professor Li Shixin. When he told the teacher, using his meager Chinese, that he loved China's martial arts and asked the teacher to take him on as a student, Professor Li answered, "Chinese martial arts are good, but practice is hard. Without the will and hard work, one cannot learn well." Then, the professor asked him to arrive at the side of a lake on campus at 5:30 the next morning. Peter did as the teacher required and was always punctual. The teacher accepted this "foreign disciple" at last. No matter the season, people can see the teacher and the student practicing Chinese martial arts in the early morning on campus. Under the teacher's guidance, Peter practiced hard to learn the basic skills. At first, his legs were as hard as tree branches and could not be pressed down as required. Then the teacher pressed legs down hard and welled up from the pain. One time, Peter was so exhausted that he could not bear it, saying, "The training is too hard." But his teacher said, "A good piece of steel is forged only after being smelted repeatedly." Peter responded, "I am willing to become good steel."

Peter studied *Taiji* Boxing, *Nanquan* Boxing, *Shaolin* Boxing, *Tanglang* Boxing, knives, sticks and *Jiujie* (nine section) whip. The *Jiujie* whip is composed of nine sections of short iron sticks connected together, with a boomerang on the top. It is a kind of soft staff and it is easy to hit oneself if one is not careful. At first, the teacher tied two thick ropes together, with two small sand bags on top to replace the whip, for fear of hurting his student. After six months of hard training, Peter mastered the essence of the nine-section whip skill. At the national martial arts competition among universities held in Shandong Province in 1997, Peter Reisman became champion of the nine-section whip. The teacher and the student have established a relationship of deep affection. Teacher Li often took Peter to take part in training by professional martial arts teams in Henan and Shandong provinces during vacations, and recommended him to participate in international martial arts competition. Peter said, "In China, teacher Li is the one who understands me most." Peter will return to the United States to study for an MBA after completing his law course at Beijing University. But he said, "I will come back to China eventually. I think I am related to China; perhaps my ancestors were Chinese."

⇡ Peter practising the nine-section whip.
↗ Good steel is forged repeatedly and good *kongfu* is gained through hard practice.
⇢ The martial arts coach Li Shixin trains his student.

↑ Teachers and classmates.
↑ Consulting with the teacher.
← Peter takes top honors in a martial arts competition.

123

↑ Taking part in a calligraphy show during his spare time.
→ "Chinese martial arts are a treasure of mankind. I will bring
  it back to the United States," said Peter.

Big Nose Nanchang Resident

◎ Photos by Zhan Xiaodong

In 1995, the U.S.-based Ford Motor Company and the Jiangling Motors Corp. Ltd. of China's Jiangxi Province established a strategic partnership to jointly manufacture Quanshun auto. John Brogen was sent to Nanchang City to act as a technical expert. John worked conscientiously and took everything seriously. One time, he found a small crack on a gasoline tank, and immediately stopped delivering the car. He personally lay on the ground to examine the crack and had all the cars examined. He said, "Not a car with quality problems should be driven out of the gate of Jiangling. Otherwise, it would influence the credibility of both Jiangling and Ford."

John has worked in the city for six years and regards himself as a Nanchang resident. If time permits, he actively takes part in the enterprise's collective activities. To better communicate with people, he learnt to speak Chinese and practiced again and again after coming back home. Helping people is a common pleasure of John and his wife. Every year, the couple goes to visit orphans in a children's welfare center. If they are too busy, they entrust friends to send their donated money to the center.

In 2001, John won the "Lushan" award issued by the People's Government of Jiangxi Province for his outstanding work. He was very happy and said, "The years spent in Nanchang are the best days in my 36-year career." He added that Nanchang people are very kind. While walking or riding in the street, he is often greeted with "Hello" or "How are you?" Whenever coming across difficulties, people always offer a hand, helping get rid of any embarrassment. John and his wife have experienced family-like warmth in Nanchang. When people asked where they came from, they gladly answered, "We are not Laowai (foreigner). We are big-nosed Nanchang residents."

Because of the work requirement, John will have to leave Nanchang. He said he felt very sad to leave the city facing such a flourishing and beautiful start. During his work in Nanchang, John witnessed the changes and development in the city. He took many photos recording these events and sent them to his friends and colleagues who once worked there to let them know something of the present Nanchang. Brogen said he would always be a good friend of Nanchang people. He would come back frequently. He and his wife would be honest visitors and invite their friends to visit this beautiful garden-like city.

127

↑ Getting ready for work.
← The couple likes to go sightseeing by bike.

⇡ Working in his office.
⇡ While touring a residential area, the couple receives
   warm welcome from kind Nanchang people.
← At the award ceremony.

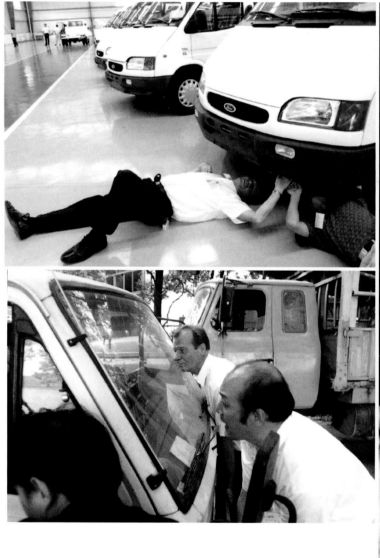

↑ Working conscientiously.
↑ Offering help on the way to work.
↗ Playing the Chinese string instrument *erhu*.

Piano Master Luca

Photos by Gu Yue

Luca, 25, comes from a small town of Italy, and is known as a musician in the local surrounding areas.

In early 2002, he came to China to teach piano in the Art School of Hainan University and studied Chinese at the same time. To get used to the life in China, he found a part-time job and worked after class in the Taihua Hotel in Haikou City. During the day, he worked as an assistant lobby manager, and, at night, he played piano and concurrently served as spare-time coach in the hotel's fitness center. He said, "I work not only for money but to contact more Chinese friends and to know more about the ordinary Chinese people's daily life, customs, and local flavor."

Luca likes to sing Chinese folk songs, and, in particular, he is keen on singing the song of *Girls of Dabancheng*, which is the first Chinese song he learnt when he came to China. This is also the song he often plays at the hotel. Sometime, he sings a Chinese folk song, although not in standard Chinese. He said that, before coming to China, he had read a story about the Chinese musician Wang Luobin and knew he was a King of Songs in the Western Region. He gained knowledge of China's music from Wang Luobin.

The Italian also likes Chinese folk culture and has a deep appreciation of China's Spring Festival. Before the Chinese New Year, the Taihua Hotel was decorated with red lanterns, red papercuts and antithetical couplets on red paper, as well as colorful fresh flowers. On New Year's Eve, all the hotel staff members and guests celebrated the festival together until the next morning, making *jiaozi*, setting off fireworks and firecrackers and watching CCTV Spring Festival Show. "It is a very interesting time. I will invite my Italian friends to China and let them experience the happy atmosphere of the Chinese Spring Festival," he said.

Luca plays Chinese folk music.
"How big these Chinese firecrackers are!"

↑ Dancing with a Chinese girl.
↑ "How delicious is Chinese rice!"
↗ On the first day of the Chinese lunar year, Luca stands at the gate of the Taihua Hotel to greet guests with "Happy New Year."

↑ Learning to drink "Kung Fu tea."
↖ Luca is a foreign language teacher for the hotel staff.

French Barbers Know China Again

There is a beauty parlor named Eric in Beijing that is run by a Frenchman. The three French barbers are 40-year-old Eric, the 27-year-old Stephane and Laurent, also 27 years old. Before coming to China, they knew very little about China and Beijing. Now, each has his unique feelings. They said they got to know China from the day when they started to serve the Chinese customers who came to have their haircut.

France is well known for its hairdressing skills. The beauty parlor shop has attracted many customers since its opening and the hairdressers have made many Chinese friends. They found that Beijing is an open and developing city full of vitality. Many Beijing residents now care very much about their hairstyle. Young people like to dye their hair in other colors, while middle-aged and old women often come for hair and skin treatment. The French hairdressers have won their customers' trust with their skill and their open-minded characteristics, rich expressions and good attitude that create a happy atmosphere.

After work, the hairdressers like to stroll around the streets. They visit the Palace Museum, and the new bars, quiet lanes and bustling downtown to experience the local flavor and make friends. They have learnt to use Chinese chopsticks and tasted real Peking roast duck, drinking and toasting happily with Beijing people. They have climbed the Tiananmen Gate Tower and toured Wangfujing Street. The three French hairdressers believe China and Beijing are developing surprisingly fast, and the vigorous city is bound to have a bright future.

An open Beijing has not only attracted French hairdressers to show their skills in the city, but also lured many wine masters, piano teachers, chefs and teachers to start their career in Beijing. Beijing residents also welcome foreign workers and live harmoniously with them. They learn from the foreign workers and jointly seek development while enjoying the services they offer.

○ Photos by Li Jinglu

↑ Stephane likes China's arts and crafts and goes to
the market whenever he has time.
↖ The three hairdressers have unique skills and they
work carefully.

† Famous Hong Kong garment designer
  Zhang Tianai enjoys Stephane's care.
→ Stephane at the Tiananmen Gate Tower.

☨ Stephane learns to use chopsticks and loves to
   eat hotpot.
☡ Stephane loves China's Peking Opera masks.
⇢ Stephane plays *zheng*, a traditional stringed
   plucked instrument.

The Westerners Street of Yangshuo

◎ Photos by Liu Jinyou

Xijie has a history of more than 1,400 years. The street is paved with marble and lined on each side by low brick and tile houses dating back to the Qing Dynasty (1644-1911). Their white walls and red wood doors and windows look simple but elegant. Xijie's flavor and customs have attracted many foreign travelers, with the annual number reaching as high as 100,000 people. Some stay form 10 days to two weeks, but others remain for six months or even a year. Karl has lived there for 10 years. Because the number of foreign visitors exceeds that of the local residents, Xijie therefore is known as "Yangren Jie" (Westerners Street).

Yangshuo City is located in the picturesque Guilin Scenic Spot. There is a saying: "Guilin's scenery is the best in the world, and Yangshuo's scenery is the best in Guilin". The mountains surrounding the city are peculiarly shaped with deep caves. The crystal clear waters of the Lijiang River flows between mountains and caves, prompting Karl to say that "Yangshuo is a paradise".

Visitors go out sightseeing on bicycles to surrounding scenic spots during the day, and, at night, they sit in front of the restaurants along Xijie Street, with candles burning, drinking beer and eating traditional Yangshuo food or sipping tea while chatting. Karl wrote a book entitled *No.58 Xijie Street*, introducing what he saw in Yangshuo. The book has attracted more German visitors after being published in Germany.

The unique scenery combining Chinese and Western cultures has also attracted TV stations, newspapers and websites at home and abroad to introduce Xijie, and many heads of state and government leaders have visited the place. Former U.S. presidents Richard Nixon, Jimmy Carter and George Bush Snr. once visited Xijie. While in office, President Bill Clinton also visited Yucun Village and Xijie where he met Mike, an American permanently living there. Clinton told him, "I know Yangshuo is your home. I really envy you."

Now more than 30 households of foreign visitors have settled in Xijie, and most of the Western food restaurants were opened by foreigners. While Chinese and Western cultures are combining, the seeds of love are also sprouting. In the last decade, there have been more than 100 marriages between Chinese and foreigners, the highest rate in China. Xijie people often visit their relatives abroad. They say proudly, "With convenient communications, going to visit overseas relatives is easier than going to the county town from the village in the past."

143

↑ On the eve of the Chinese New Year, three French visitors listen to old Yangshuo folk music in a small restaurant.
↑ Grandma can also speak a little foreign language with foreign visitors.
← Old but young Xijie Street.

FOREIGNERS IN CHINA

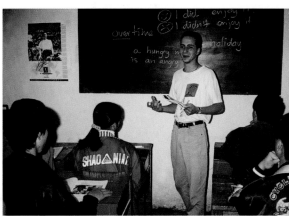

144

↑ Martin, from Switzerland, teaches at the Xijie foreign Languages School.

↑ Two foreign visitors praise the street folk craftsman for his animal art products weaved with palm leaves.

→ When the curtain of darkness falls, restaurants in Xijie move dining tables out to let foreign visitors from different countries enjoy the local food.

⇑ China's martial arts have a long history, and can both help people keep fit and understand local culture.

⇑ "When in Rome do as the Romans do."

⇗ Buying a Chinese national costume.

⇒ A couple from Canada gather together with their relatives and friends to hold their wedding ceremony in Xijie.

图书在版编目(CIP)数据

外国人在中国／焦波编.
－北京：五洲传播出版社，2003.12
ISBN 7-5085-0384-8
I.外···
II.焦···
III.外国人－生活－状况－中国－画册－英文
IV.D669-64
中国版本图书馆 CIP 数据核字(2003)第 120703 号

序　　言：李　莎（加拿大）
撰　　文：苏晓环
责任编辑：焦　波
图片编辑：胡艳丽
翻　　译：潘双琴
英文审稿：李　莎（加拿大）
校　　对：张行军
装帧设计：田　林　傅晓斌
制　　作：北京原色印象文化艺术中心

外国人在中国

出版发行：五洲传播出版社
通讯地址：中国北京北三环中路 31 号
邮政编码：100088
电　　话：8610-82008174 83793335
网　　址：www.cicc.org.cn
印　　刷：北京华联印刷有限公司
开　　本：1/16　889 × 1194
印　　张：9.25
版　　次：2003 年 12 月第一版 2003 年 12 月第一次印刷
书　　号：ISBN 7-5085-0384-8/D · 168
定　　价：140 元